MANDALAS
WITH FLOWERS & VEGETATION

THIS BOOK BELONGS TO:

....

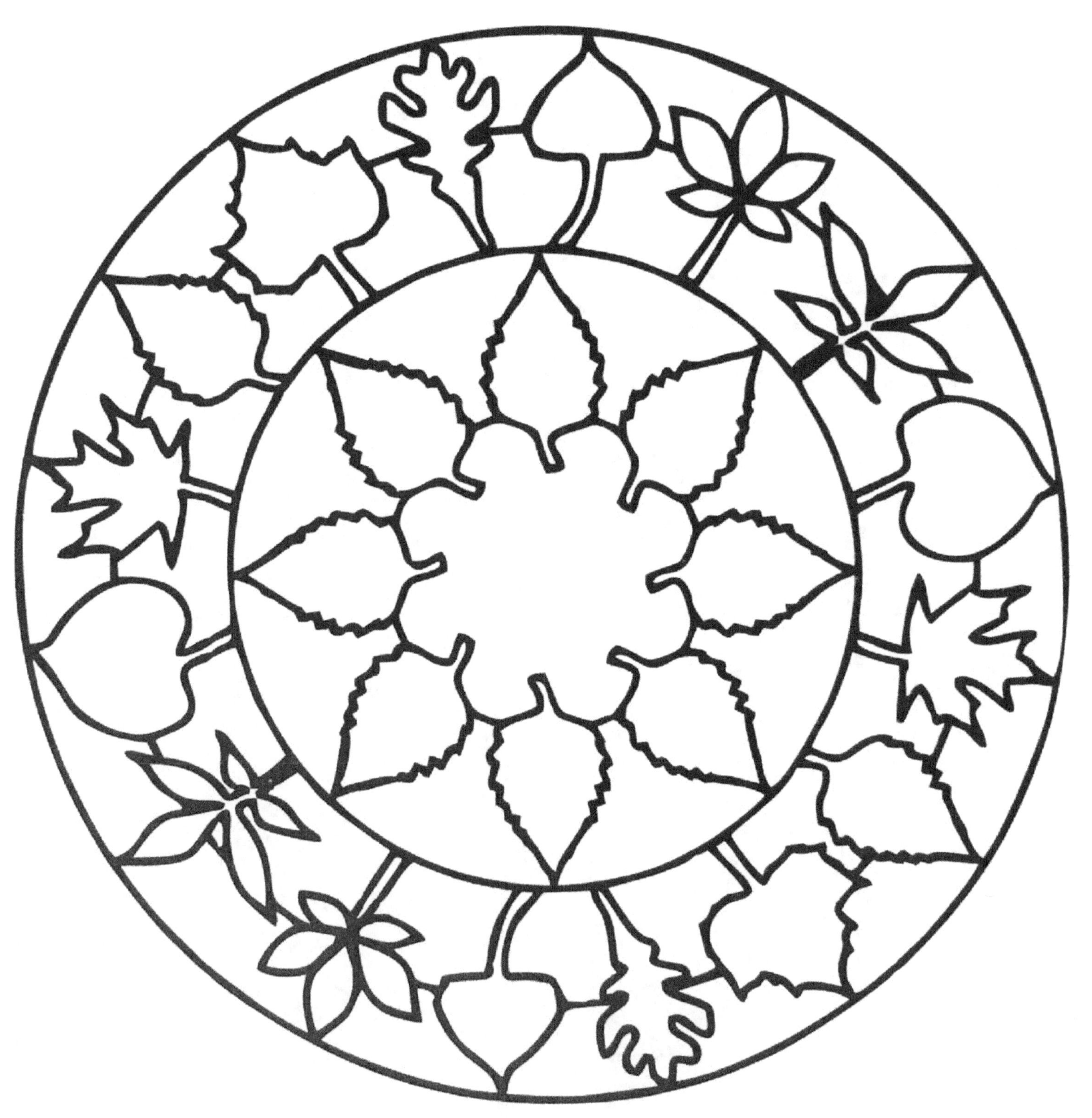

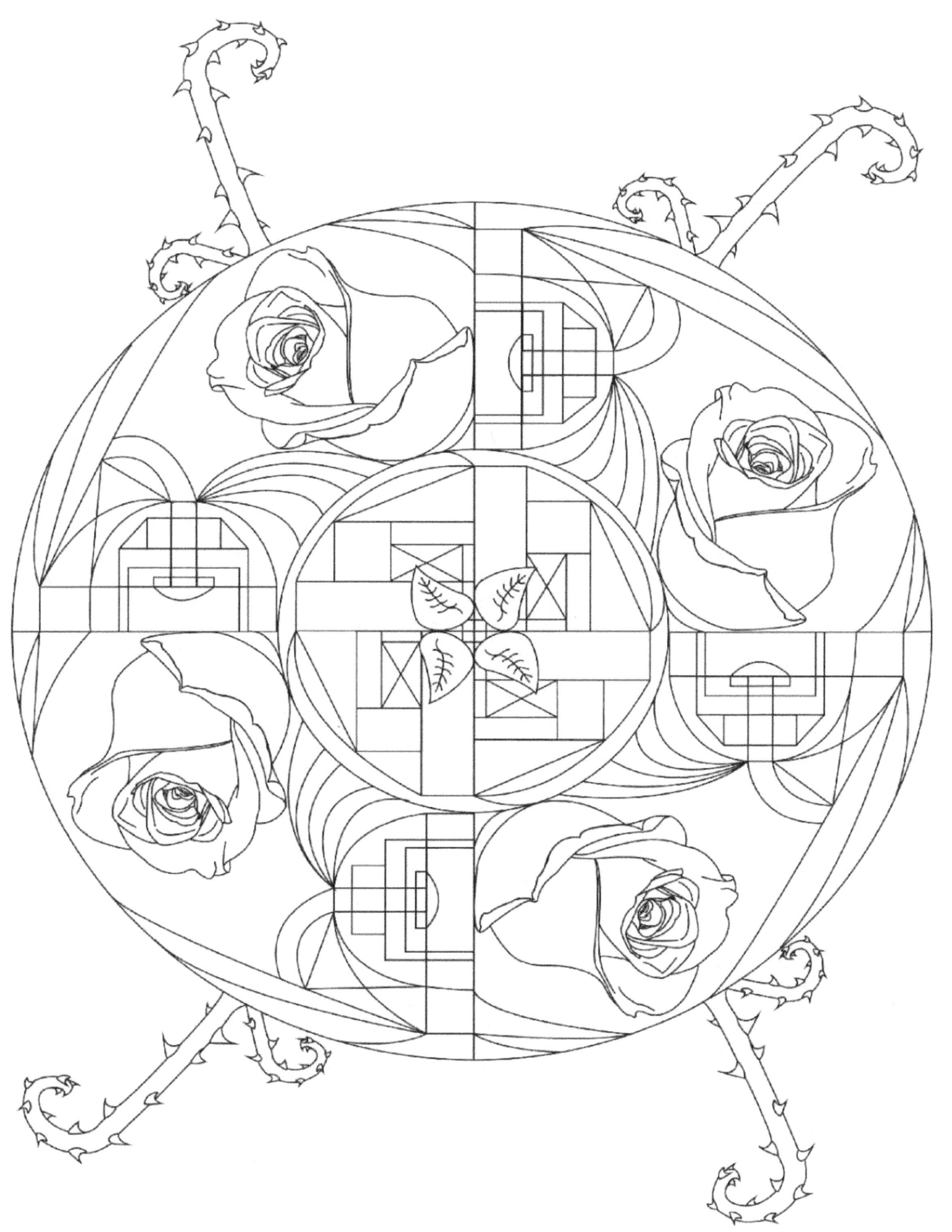

LE BONHEUR EST UN CHAMP QUI ONDULE SOUS LE VENT ET QUI POUSSE SES RACINES DANS UN SOL QUI NOURRIT

www.ingramcontent.com/pod-product-compliance
Lightning Source LLC
Chambersburg PA
CBHW081418250726
48654CB00013B/1744